FOREWORD BY SOFIA COPPOLA

INTRODUCTION BY GREGORY CREWDSON

EDITED BY ROBERT HARSHORN SHIMSHAK

leisure *BILL OWENS*

fotofolio

I have really been influenced by photography, especially the work of Bill Owens. I first saw Bill's photos in a gallery in San Francisco with my mom. She bought me the image of the kids at a school dance under foil stars, and this image, along with many others from *Suburbia*, became visual references for my first movie, *The Virgin Suicides*. I love how he focuses in on the banal details of life and how he captures seventies American suburbia both as a participant in that world and an outsider at the same time. Here is *Leisure*, the next chapter of his work as a great American observer.

SOFIA COPPOLA

A PARTICULAR KIND OF STRANGENESS

A family of three carefully unfolds rolls of sod onto their barren front yard transforming it into a small domestic oasis.

A man ascends a bare, undersized tree in an absurd attempt to prune its dead leaves.

A young boy sits on his Big Wheel holding a toy rifle while staring menacingly at the camera.

Bill Owens made these photographs, and many others, in various suburban communities in Northern California throughout the early 1970s. In 1973 they were compiled in the classic book, *Suburbia*. These photographs are as strange and compelling now as they were thirty years ago. Over the next two decades he continued his chronicles on American life with the equally strong and insightful books *Our Kind of People* (1975), *Working – I do it for the Money* (1977), and now this final volume in the loosely knit series, *Leisure* (2004). Owens' photographs belong to an American aesthetic tradition of art that explores the intersection of everyday life and theatricality. Like the paintings of Edward Hopper, the photographs of Walker Evans and Diane Arbus, and the short stories of John Cheever and Raymond Carver, Owens' photographs find unexpected beauty and mystery within the American vernacular. This collision between normality and strangeness transforms the American landscape into a place of wonder and anxiety.

Owens is among the generation of photographers, including Robert Adams, William Eggleston, Steven Shore, and Joel Sternfeld, who used the tradition of documentary photography to explore the complexities and contradictions of the American landscape. To varying degrees, they used an objective style of photography in an effort to locate a perfect tension between banality and beauty, domesticity and nature, criticism and admiration.

Bill Owens' photographic sensibility is straightforward and direct. He approached the subject of suburbia and its inhabitants in an almost non-descript style. This neutrality is, of course, deceptive. Collectively, the photographs reveal a highly subjective and complex narrative viewpoint. The pictures oscillate between irony and admiration, absurdity and sadness, and truth and fiction. Quotidian settings like the home, the yard, the club, the workplace or the vacation spot serve as backdrops in which small events are played out in front of the camera. Owens' photographs use telling details, odd occurrences, and quiet revelations to transform these familiar scenes into small dramas.

For me, the strongest characteristic in these photographs is their particular kind of strangeness. Owens pictures suburbia as a place of comfort and stability. However, he searches beneath the veneer of domestic trappings and uncovers an undercurrent of repressed anxiety, alienation and sexual desire. There is an extraordinary sense of dislocation in these photographs. The subjects who inhabit these pictures appear dislocated from their families, their neighbors, their homes, their possessions, and finally, from themselves.

Bill Owens' photographs have shaped a generation of young artists, filmmakers, writers, and photographers. His influence is evident in a wide range of contemporary artists including filmmakers Paul Thomas Anderson, Wes Anderson, Sofia Coppola and Todd Solondz, writers A.M. Homes and Rick Moody, painters John Currin and Lisa Yuskavage, and photographers Jenny Gage, Katy Grannan, and Malerie Marder. These artists, who all came of age in the 1990s, share a distanced fascination with 1970s style, fashion, and décor. Their interest in this subject matter comes not from direct experience, but from a vast reservoir of existing images and representations. For a generation of artists, Bill Owens' photographs define the iconography of the 1970s. The *Suburbia* series has become part of our cultural lexicon.

GREGORY CREWDSON

7   Every summer we go all out on our camp in Yosemite. I do the barbecuing.

The last thing I did before leaving for San Francisco after my dad died was watch fireworks explode over the St. Louis arch on the Fourth of July. Two days later I crested a hill on Route 80 and saw the expanse of San Francisco Bay for the first time. It was so beautiful I cried.

As Snowbirds we winter in Arizona and summer in Montana. KOA makes it possible to travel cheaply.

At the Livermore Air Show we sit around doing nothing. Everybody coming by wants to talk about stunt flying.

My dream is to drive a car at Indy. This is as close as I'll get.

At night we froze the raccoons in our flashlight as they tried to get at the food we hung high in the air on a line. Janet put her contact lenses in a plastic bread bag for safekeeping but as we were waking up in the morning a fox darted through the campsite, snatched the bag and ran away. I never knew camping could be so exciting.

On the weekends the traffic is always bumper to bumper just like a commute day. You drive for four hours to look at El Capitan for four minutes, and most people never get out of the car.

I'm here to meet boys.

I am hot to trot.

When school is out we sunbathe all day and dance all night.

I had over 4,000 cacti plants in my garden including 3,000 different varieties. Clubs would ask to see my collection. I gave small tours to people in the hope of forming a local cactus and succulent society, but there was not enough interest. Last year, all the neighbors around me watered their lawns so much that it killed many of my plants, so I had to sell the entire collection to an orchid grower in Carmichael.

I spent $100 on the plane kit and 50 hours assembling it. My goal is not to crash it in the first ten minutes.

On weekends we camp and ride dirt bikes.

My husband's job allows a lot of vacation time. This allows us to go to the lake.

We answered an ad in the newspaper to have our picture taken doing yoga. We feel it is so easy and natural to pose.

Tai Chi Chuen is an old form of Chinese exercise. It involves meditation and loosening of the body muscles for blood circulation and concentration. Tai Chi is good for relaxation in our society of hustle-bustle.

Karate is a highly competitive sport, like tennis or boxing. It's one on one. For $30 a month a kid can get some good mental and physical training. He can learn coordination, balance, timing and self-defense.

Lawn bowling is for old men with too much time on their hands.

I took up golf when I retired. It gets me out of the house and away from my wife who always wants me to do something else.

I only play croquet once a year on the Fourth of July. The rest of the day we spend at the neighbors' pool drinking beer.

Everywhere we go we challenge the local high school team to a game. We let them win. It's all for charity. Points don't count unless you shoot from the back of the donkey. Donkeys are dumb and uncooperative, and they really hate to move.

Kids today are so mobile. They all have their own cars. I cannot believe there is a sixteen-year-old kid who drives a new Mercedes 450SL to school.

The Raiders are my team. The fans here aren't stuck up like those across the bay. We like to work ourselves up in the parking lot during the tailgate party with a few beers then really cuss out the visiting team.

We came because George Plimpton was invited, but he didn't show up.

Nowadays you even have to stand in line to exercise.

The three of us, we have made over one thousand jumps with no malfunctions. We love the sport of sky diving.

It's called hot air balloon races but, really, how can you race a balloon?

The soccer league is administered by a self-appointed group of parents who have become great soccer enthusiasts. They decided it was time to divide the players according to their abilities by creating a Red Division for the better athletes and a White Division for the also-rans. There were a lot of parents who didn't want the stigma of their sons being in the White Division. They didn't want to go to the supermarket and have to explain to their neighbors that their kids weren't competitive. If a boy gets the impression he is not as good as little Joey who's in the Red Division, this will scar his mental image of himself as an achiever in life.

My goal at the end of the race is to beat at least one ten-year-old kid or one little old lady.

I first got interested in hockey when I lived back east. Its speed, sounds, violence, and the beautiful choreographed motion got to me. The Seals are one of the worst teams in the league and only really dedicated fans come. Sometimes when good teams visit, there are more fans rooting for them than for the home team. I love them anyway.

When I started dirt bike racing there were hardly any spectators. It was for the love of the sport. Now thousands come hoping they will see a spectacular crash.

Field Day at our school pits the girls against the boys. The boys are stronger, but we are more determined to win.

I learned how to juggle while doing porn films. I needed something to kill time during takes. Some
days us extras do nothing at all.

Keep our city clean – eat a pigeon.

The Amateur Athletic Union swim meets are held on weekends year round – summer and winter. A typical meet in Class B will have 3,000 entries competing in the backstroke, breaststroke, freestyle and the butterfly. Some 300 families will come to watch and officiate the meet. Swimming is a sport where boys and girls are trained and coached together. The only division is their abilities.

In the daytime the staff plays volleyball with the guests. At night they smoke dope.

I rode my motorcycle as far as I could and then walked into the Rolling Stones Altamont concert with 300,000 other people. I climbed the sound tower with my Nikon, three lenses, a sandwich and a jar of water. The first group on the stage was Grace Slick and the Jefferson Airplane. Soon a guy climbed the tower with a pipe wrench and threatened me if I didn't come down. Later that night, the Hell's Angels killed a man in the audience. By then, I was home.

Most of these dogs have trainers and travel seven months each year from show to show. The owners seldom attend the shows. All they want are the trophies.

Judges can be very fickle and unfair.

Kiss me. Kiss me.

I'm just killing time.

When your son is a Cub Scout and is given a block of pine wood and told to make a six-ounce racing car, you know good old dad does the work. And of course, at the Pine Wood Derby race dad races the cars. But your son gets a trophy and gets to keep the car on a shelf in his bedroom.

You have no idea how stupid I felt talking to one of the sculptures.

74

Everywhere Sam goes heads turn. He is a God here in Los Angeles.

Is my husband Franco trying to tell me something I don't want to hear?

The title is so appropriate. Where else would I put it?

After work we change clothes, redo our makeup, do some coke and go dancing.

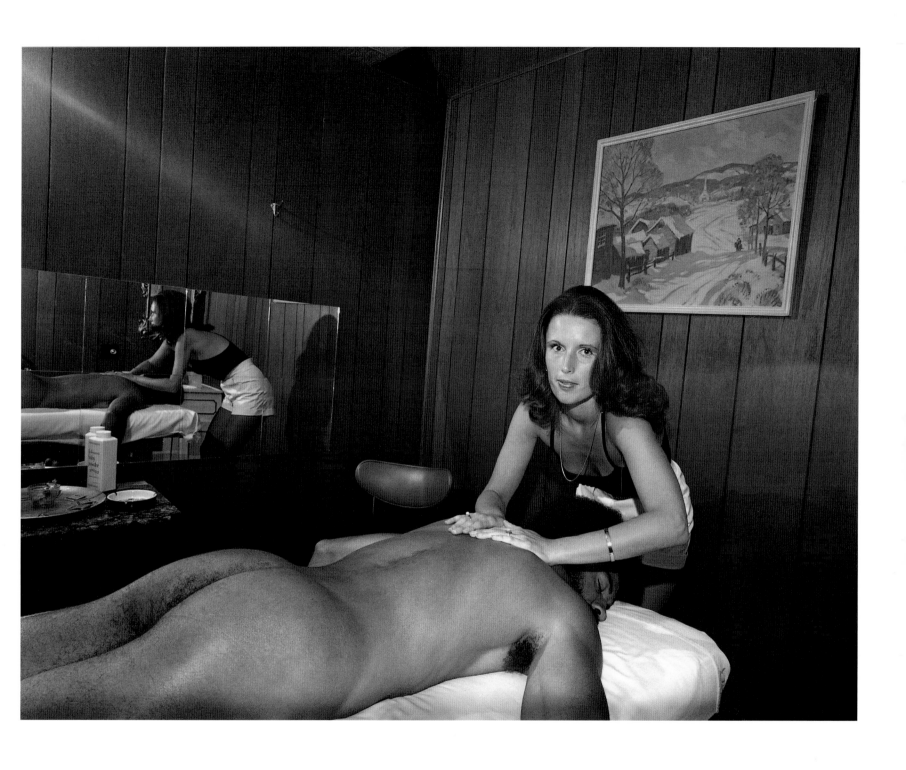

Massage opens up the soul. That's why I chose it as a profession. I also make good money.

I don't know why I bought another wig. What I really needed was some deck furniture.

Thirty years ago the Rebecca Women's Club would have a turkey whist card party. It would bring out 250 players. Today we're lucky to get 50. That's with prizes, too. Maybe a turkey isn't worth as much as it used to be.

The Eagle Squares is one of 100 clubs in the Northern California Square Dancing Association. We called our group Eagle Squares because we used to dance in the Eagles Hall. My wife and I started when some neighbors talked us into taking a beginning square dance class. We found dancing to be good clean fun, something we could do together with little expense involved.

Kids aren't interested in canning or making pickles. It's hard to keep the class's attention.

For his fifth birthday I took my son Max and his six friends to the Ringling Brothers circus at the Oakland Coliseum. It was all I could do to keep them under control and not lose anyone in the crowd. As party favors I bought each of them battery-powered plastic swords with flame blades and dragons on the handles. It was easy to find them as the sword blades glowed in the dark.

It was a total scam. The really big rats were stuffed.

Our Chinese New Year meal ended with the traditional opening of the fortune cookie. Mine said, "beware of the unexpected." A moment later I bit into my cookie and a filling fell out of my teeth. The filling disappeared down my throat and it lodged in a very sensitive place. It ruined my whole evening.

When I was a child I learned to play Mah Jongg from my mother and her two sisters. They had a beautiful boxed set with tiles made of ivory that I liked to use as building blocks. In those days, every Jewish mother played. Now all the players are middle-aged or old like me.

I read every chance I get.

My witness is here for Jehovah. Usually people walk by, but if you catch someone's eye they will stop and take the magazine.

I was disappointed. This movie didn't show any sex.

McDonald's modern day care center keeps the boys out of my hair and lets me have a moment to myself.

The Livermore Independent newspaper office was upstairs and the biker bar was downstairs. I never went into the bar. I drank beer at home.

It was a total madhouse, but I would do anything to see the Bee Gees.

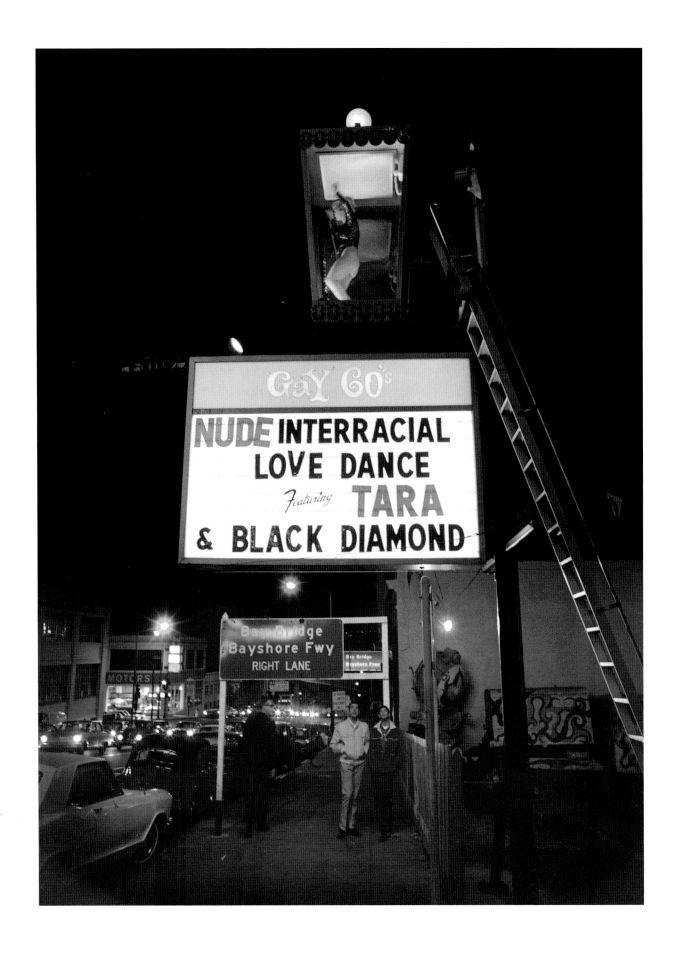

At Rosie O'Grady's Goodtime Emporium the music is provided by a Dixieland jazz band.

It's a matter of pride and I like to gamble. We roll to see who pays for the drinks.

I do what I want to do, and I don't care what the neighbors do.

The middle class has no taste for art! I am not a great artist, but people think I am because I have long hair.

I have to keep in shape. It's hard work being a realtor.

My Chinese cooking classes are divided into two groups, beginning and advanced. That's people with beginning tastes and those who will try anything. Everyone wants to know how to cook Peking duck or make 1000-year-old eggs.

For my husband's 84th birthday I bought him the girl in the cake. He was thrilled to death and we were afraid he might have another heart attack.

Learning to pack your suitcase properly for a trip is something everyone needs to learn but never does. If your bag weighs too much, or you bring the wrong clothes it can ruin your whole trip.

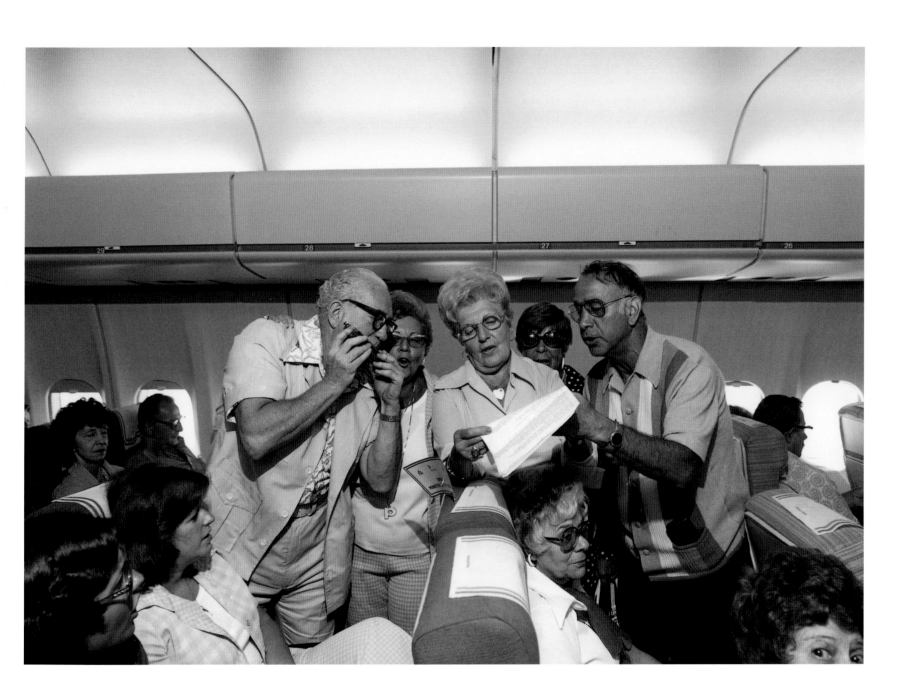

Our singing group will take any opportunity to perform, especially if it's a captive audience.

My dream is to have a cabin in the mountains.

DEDICATION:
This book is dedicated to Robert Harshorn Shimshak, whose persistence and encouragement made it a reality. I am deeply grateful to Martin Bondell, Juliette Galant, Ron Schick, Suzanne Barker, and the team at Fotofolio for the many years of support and faith in my work, and the beautiful design of both *Leisure* and *Suburbia*. Special thanks to Libby McCoy for making the wonderful prints that bring life to these photographs.

Larry Sultan took my picture as a baseball player for a set of playing cards of well-known photographers that would mimic sports cards. I chose to have the picture taken at my home in the cactus garden wearing cowboy boots for protection. My batting average that year was a 1,000 because I had just gotten a Guggenheim Award.

© 2004 by Bill Owens
www.billowens.com

Fotofolio
561 Broadway
New York, New York 10012

Printed in China
Library of Congress Control Number: 2004112459
ISBN: 1-58418-074-9 (hardcover)

0106,44,77